Lighthouse

Lindy

Lighthouse Lindy

Gloria D. Butler

Illustrations by Laura Shanley

Lighthouse Lindy
Copyright © 2008 Gloria D. Butler
Published by Arbor Books, Inc.

All rights reserved. No part of this book may be reproduced (except for inclusion in reviews), disseminated or utilized in any form or by any means, electronic or mechanical, including photocopying, recording, or in any information storage and retrieval system, or the Internet/World Wide Web without written permission from the author or publisher.

For further information, please contact:
gloriabutler@mac.com

Book design by:
Arbor Books Inc.
www.arborbooks.com

Printed in the United States of America

Lighthouse Lindy
Gloria D. Butler

Illustrations by Laura Shanley

1. Title 2. Author 3. Children

Library of Congress Control Number: 2007921077

ISBN 10: 0-9790469-6-3
ISBN 13: 978-0-9790469-6-4

*Dedicated to
my miracle son,
Patrick,
Born August 16, 1993.*

You are my heart and soul, my inspiration and my blessing. You are a very special gift from God, not only to me, but to the world.

Through all of life's storms, remember to stand strong, be dependable, never give up your dreams and be proud not because of what you have, but who you are.

God is doing very wonderful work in and through you, so follow his light and you will always shine.

With all my heart and love,

Mom

Lighthouse Lindy

Lindy sat calmly overlooking the massive, aqua-blue ocean that stretched before her. It was one of those balmy days when tropical breezes swayed the stately palm trees and seagulls swooped low over the water in search of food. During the summer, tropical storms could pop up at the drop of a hat, so Lindy had to stay alert and keep careful watch on the sailors at sea. Boats, speckling the horizon, always kept at least one eye toward Lindy's light so they could see the way back to shore quickly, if needed.

She was the only lighthouse for miles around. For years, she had worked day and night so travelers at sea could find their way home. She knew all the sailors were depending on her. It felt good to be needed. Into the harbor, ships would come as the white-capped waves hid them from view one minute and pushed them to the top of the crest the next.

Salty, as the locals called him, knew Lindy better than anyone. The old man had been sailing these southern waters many years and knew in a flash how quickly a serene sea could turn into a violent beast against a shrimper such as himself. But, he also knew that Lindy would always be there to show him the way back home.

Lindy loved her job. She wasn't very tall. In fact, she was rather short and stocky for a lighthouse. Her white paint was a little chipped. Her windows had a few cracks. But still, she mustered all her strength to shine brightly night and day for her sailors. She loved pretty days when families would come and picnic beside her while watching the beautiful waters dance. She smiled as she saw the children play. Her bright eyes sparkled with joy and glittered across the turquoise water. She especially loved the feeling of helping people, and felt she had the very best job and the very best home in the entire world. It didn't matter to her if she wasn't the prettiest or didn't have the newest things—she felt good about herself and who she was.

Until one day…

It was early morning when she awakened to the sound of bulldozers clearing the land on the cliff across the channel.

"What's going on over there?" wondered Lindy. "Maybe I'm getting a new neighbor. I sure hope he's cute," she thought with a wink of her light. It wasn't long before concrete was poured and builders began to construct a tall frame.

"Hmmm," thought Lindy. "If I didn't know better, I'd think that a lighthouse was being built over there, although a much taller one than me. But no, it couldn't be. I mean… I'm here. I do a great job and we certainly don't need two lighthouses on this shore. I have helped a lot of people. I don't need any help."

She quickly tried to put it out of her mind and continued to let her little gas light shine. But day by day, she sat there, constantly reminded that she was going to have to share her beach and wondering what would be next door.

Then, it happened. Her fears were confirmed. She saw a huge light, bigger than any she had ever seen, being placed in the top. It was different from her small gas light. It had a lot of wires and was connected to something with lots of buttons and switches.

Lindy had never actually seen a computer, but she figured a light that big must be operated by one. She wished she had a computer with all those pretty buttons. Then, almost before she knew what was happening, Patrick, her faithful friend and lighthouse keeper, shut off her light. With tears in his eyes, he slowly pulled the door closed and looked back sadly at Lindy as he left.

"What's happening to me?" Lindy wondered. Did I do something wrong? Why don't they like me anymore?" A wave of sadness and a little jealousy washed over her as she looked now from her dark but always faithful windows toward the tall, beautiful lighthouse on the rock beside her. All night, Lindy questioned why she had been replaced.

After finally falling into a restless sleep, she awoke to sounds of a celebration coming from the cliff belonging to her new and unwelcomed neighbor. A group of people had gathered around the black-and-white-striped light, which was wrapped in the biggest red bow she had ever seen—much bigger than the bows little girls would wear in their hair when they would come for a visit.

A band was playing and it looked as if everyone in town had clamored out to see the newest and most handsome lighthouse ever. Then, a man, who looked like the mayor, cut the red ribbon to officially open the new lighthouse.

Even though Lindy thought that she had never seen such a big, bright light, her heart ached with the feeling that she was no longer needed. She knew she had as much to offer as any other lighthouse and didn't understand what had happened.

"What's going to happen to me? Are they going to tear me down, or make me stay up here forever all by myself? Will I ever see Patrick again? I miss him. I miss the sound of children playing and seeing families watching the sunset beside me," Lindy thought sadly.

The new lighthouse, Laramie, stood tall and quite proud of his new job. He'd glance over to Lindy from time to time, chuckling to himself, "What a frail little fat lighthouse. I'm so much better than her. Look at her tattered paint and cracked windows. She's even still using a gas lamp, but I have the latest in computer technology running my light. I'm wearing fashionable stripes and she's wearing plain ol' white. My windows are clear and I have fresh flowers decorating my grounds. What a joke she is!" Laramie laughed to himself.

Before long, summer days turned to fall. Mid-September brought the worst of the hurricane season.

Laramie couldn't wait to prove that he was the best lighthouse ever. He just knew that his light could reach sailors farther than Lindy ever could.

As sure as the sun rises and sets, the season's first major storm was announced. Hurricane Adam aimed its sights on the pretty coastal town.

Lindy wished so much that she could help the sailors she had grown to love over the years. She felt helpless as she watched Laramie beam, while she just sat there in the dark and watched.

Hurricane warnings sounded. Sailors set sail back to port as quickly as they could, but some still got caught in the rain bands and tropical winds that preceded the eye of the storm. Night came and suddenly it was showtime for Laramie. He puffed up his light and was ready to be the town hero. Hurricane-force winds began to howl, and a forty-foot tidal surge crashed violently over the shore, knocking out all power across the town. But, where was Laramie? Why wasn't he shining for the sailors? Lindy looked frantically toward the rocks beside her and he was sitting in total darkness.

"Oh, no!" Lindy thought. "The winds from Adam must have knocked out the power to Laramie's light. Computers can't run without electricity. The builders must have thought Laramie was fool-proof and didn't even install a generator to keep him going." Meanwhile, Patrick was wondering what to do while he paced the floor at his nearby home. "Only a miracle could help the sailors now," thought Patrick. "Only a miracle…the small but reliable gas-powered miracle named Lindy."

As quick as lightning, Patrick dashed out into the hurricane-force winds toward his faithful friend. Laramie, now sitting embarrassed by the whole thing, was ashamed of all his boasting. "How could this happen to me?" he thought.

Sailors continued to be tossed around on forty-foot waves searching frantically and aimlessly for some light on the horizon that would show them the way home.

Captain Salty's boat, the SS Fish & Chips, found itself smashed against a rock. Fishermen scrambled out of the boat and helped each other to safety.

Lindy sat watching the horrible scene unfold before her, not knowing that Patrick was on his way. "Oh, how terrible for those poor people to be out there in the dark," she thought. "If only I could turn on my light, I could help save them."

No sooner had she thought it than she heard the door at her base creak open and the sound of familiar footsteps running quickly up her stairs. "Hi, Lindy ol' girl. I've missed you so much!" exclaimed Patrick. "You wouldn't believe the mess out there tonight! You've got to help bring the sailors back home. Laramie couldn't do it. I told them not to shut you down. Now, they'll see how wrong they were about you. You may not have everything Laramie has, but you've always been a faithful friend to the sailors just the way you are."

Patrick lit Lindy's gas light. Suddenly, as quickly as it had gone out, Lindy felt a warmth flow through her again—not only from her light, but also in her heart. Sailors radioed that they finally saw the light and were headed home.

Lindy never felt better. Her sadness vanished and her smile returned as her light once again danced across the stormy waters, toward the desperate eyes of the fishermen. The next day, people from all over the town rushed back to see their faithful friend and repay Lindy for a job well done. Men cut weeds and repaired her broken glass. Women scraped off the old, chipped paint and repainted Lindy the way she used to be: bright, cheery and radiant. Once again, children came to run and play up and down her stairs. Their laughter even caused Lindy to chuckle.

As she sat there smiling to herself, Lindy overheard the mayor say, "You know, fancier and newer isn't always better. Last night, we saw that."

"It's who you are, not what you have. Real beauty comes from the heart," said the mayor. "From now on, Lindy will be cherished forever as a vital part of our community. Our children and grandchildren will sail under her watchful light for years to come."

As for Lindy, never again will she question her own worth or value. She feels good about herself again, even though she still doesn't have all the latest, fancy gadgets of other modern lighthouses. She has learned to forgive Laramie and to accept his differences.

As for Laramie, he's learned that having more didn't make him a better lighthouse. He's been humbled by Lindy's sweet, simple spirit and determination. City officials have decided that Laramie, too, is still a valuable part of the community, so they gave him a gift of a new generator to prevent any problems in the future. They both have learned that while working alone is great, working as a team is even better. They've learned that forgiveness and friendship are what's really important, not what someone has. You don't often see two lighthouses working so closely together, but today that's exactly what Lindy and Laramie are doing. They sit across the channel from each, other letting their lights dance over the waters, directing the boats into the mouth of the channel and safely back home.

A letter Lindy sent to you, the reader:

Dear new friend,

If you have a dream, follow it . Don't let anyone discourage you or get down on yourself because you don't have everything someone else has. You've got all you need to accomplish great things—your heart and your desire. If you stay faithful to what you believe in and shine brightly where you are now, doors will open for you.

I love you,

Lindy

P.S. I'll keep my light lit and will be watching for yours in the distance!

"You are the light of the world—like a city on a mountain, glowing in the night for all to see."

—Matthew 5:14